SUCCESS
IN REAL ESTATE
AND THE ART OF
STAYING IN BUSINESS

Vicky Keeton

Real Estate Broker

ISBN: 1-4392-4573-8
ISBN-13: 9781439245736

Visit www.booksurge.com to order additional copies.

Limit of Liability and Disclaimer of Warranty.

This book is dedicated to:

To my sister Paula who sent me countless customers and never stopped believing in me, thank-you. To my best friend, Neil, who spent endless nights listening to me, thank-you, and thank-you, Blair, for the three years of hard work as my assistant.
Most of all, I dedicate this book to my three children, Pamela, Carla, and Glenn.

I Love All of You!

LET US BE LESS JUDGING AND MORE OBSERVING

I have found that if I pay attention to the people and events that come into my
life,
listen to what they have to say,
see how and if it fits my needs
or how it feels in my heart,
then my life flows smoothly
because all that I need is given to me through them.

Vicky February 2009[1]

---

1 Source Microsoft Clip Art, animals, birds, feathers, nature. Scalable, 19KB, JPJ

TABLE OF CONTENTS

MY STORY

Wow, I would soon turn fifty and doing a lot of thinking about my life, which had been something of a struggle. I had raised three children—for eighteen years as a single mom. I had thirty years' of accounting and secretarial work on my résumé, but I absolutely hated my job. I was eager for a change but had no idea what shape that change should take. I just knew that it was definitely time to make a better life for myself.

My circumstances weren't the best for making a big change. I had no savings. The $10,000 in my 401(K) was the only money I could get my hands on quickly. My car was paid for, but my house note was $1,200.00 per month. If I had given a bit more thought to what I was planning, I would never have done it. I think there comes a time in life when you just have to make a decision and go for it. I did.

I felt a need to go to a retreat in Maui, Hawaii, but I didn't have the money. That Christmas I received a Delta buddy pass that would cover the cost of airfare. All I needed was the $1,500.00 seminar fee. Then I wrecked my car. That may seem like a setback, but the damage was minimal, so I used the insurance money to pay my seminar fee. (Later, two people came into my life, and I was able to have my car repaired at very little cost. Things really do have a way of working out.) I was on my way.

Taking that trip turned out to be the best decision of my life. I began a journey that changed, and continues to change, my life. I did a lot of soul work at that seminar and a lot of healing. It transformed everything!

During one of the classes, a lady turned to me and said, "You have such charisma. You really need to be in real estate." I was intrigued; that woman didn't even know me, and she was suggesting a path for my future. Was I being led to a career? Yes, I believe I was. After returning home, I saw a sign for free real estate classes, this gave me an idea to once again explore a career in real estate and I embarked on a new life. I had been in real estate when my children were young, and because I had held my license for three years (this is the requirement to apply for your brokers license) I was eligible to take my brokers exam which allowed me to receive my brokers. However, I started my career as an Associate Broker.

I turned in my notice at the job I hated and never looked back. It turned out to be one of the best decisions I have ever made. But in the beginning…wow…the fear set in. You take a class to get a license to sell real estate, but they do not teach you *how* to sell real estate. You have to figure that out for yourself. Until now.

I was petrified. I was a single woman with only $10,000.00 and no income. Until I made a sale, that $10,000 was the only thing between me and the wolf at the door. I did the math and realized that with my house note and regular expenses the money would not last long. It didn't.

One of the first things I did was listen and learn from the experience of top-producing agents who could answer my questions and offer guidance as to the best way to get started in this business. As we all know experience is a great teacher. Next, I bought a book on how to list and sell real estate. I needed to learn quickly and didn't want to reinvent the wheel. The book helped, but I noticed a lot of the ideas didn't work for me. Many of the suggestions I received from brokers and media were no longer viable because these people were no longer in the business of selling real estate and didn't understand the issues of the current market and needs of our customers and clients. Some of the seminars and training sessions I attended were great, but the accompanying material was expensive. Often they suggested using scripts when approaching potential clients but I could not bring myself to use a fake persona and read someone else's words.

However, the book shared a lot of secrets for how to walk a subdivision. I decided that I could stay home on Saturday mornings and get depressed, or I could walk subdivisions, get exercise, and introduce myself to people. Wow, what a gift! I listed and sold thirteen homes in the first subdivision I walked. People loved the fact that I was willing to walk their subdivision and meet them face to face. They said if I was going to put forth that much effort, they knew I would sell their homes. I *did*.

Within six months I was up and running. From that point forward, I continually improved my approach for marketing, listing, and selling real estate. I was in the top ten in my office almost every month, and one year I was listed in ReMax Greater Atlanta's top twenty-five agents in Georgia.

This book is about becoming successful. I found the more organized I was, the more customers I could handle. In the process, I became a different person. I love my customers, and they reward me with referrals. My business today is almost all referrals. It just goes to show you that if you work the process, it will work for you.

My proven program will lead you to success! Above all—have fun!

Nine years after I took that first step toward a better life, I have my own company and have written and marketed my first publication. Next, I plan to write my life story. Stay tuned.

Vicky

CHAPTER 1
THE BASICS

SUCCESS IN REAL ESTATE

1) Incorporate
   You can use a certified public accountant (CPA, attorney, or you can do it yourself online at http://www.sos.*yourstate*.gov/Corporations/. Incorporating allows you to reduce your tax burden and personal liability.

2) Pay yourself a monthly salary and set up a quarterly draw. Your salary needs to be in proportion to your sales income. Your CPA can offer guidance about the appropriate amounts and explain the tax implications.

3) Pay your taxes quarterly.
   *Depending on your income or if you have an assistant, you may need to pay your taxes monthly.

4) Set up an accounting system to track expenses.
   *One of the most cost-effective solutions I found was to rent a professional printer for approximately $142.00 per month which includes all your ink (cost and quantity details may vary from state to state).

5) Set up a line of credit to offset fluctuation in the real estate market. This allows you to always have available cash, which promotes a feeling of **confidence** and **prosperity** instead of desperation and fear.

Over the years, I found that in order to run my business successfully,

I HAD TO RUN IT AS AN ACTUAL

BUSINESS!

SETTING UP YOUR SYSTEMS: THE BASICS

1) Write down the names, addresses, and phone numbers of at least 100 people you know. This is where your leads and first customers will come from. This is the beginning of setting up your referral business. And this is the greatest resource you will ever have.
   a) Doctor, dentist, relatives, friends, and business acquaintances, etc.

2) Enter these people and their contact information into your database.
   a) Print these labels to mail out your monthly newsletters.
   b) Print out their contact information and carry it with you. This will allow you to arrange visits with your customers when you are in their area.

3) Use the Web site https://toolbox.orhp.com/ to produce customized, professional-looking newsletters that you can print and mail monthly. My customers enjoy reading all the articles that are provided in these newsletters. Just print and send. I suggest that you rent a postage machine to make the mailing process easier.

4) As you meet with new contacts (potential customers), immediately enter their names, addresses, and phone numbers into your database.

5) Purchase two white boards and label one board Listings and the other board Sales. These will help you keep track of your listings and sales. For inspiration, I put a Sold sign above my listing board. Use whatever motivates you.

6) Set up twelve folders labeled January through December. As you close each sale, enter all pertinent information onto the anniversary tract sheet (see forms #1) and include a copy of the listing. As the next year comes you will need this information to complete your yearly comparative market analysis (CMA) (more on this in buyers section). Label one folder End of Year (EOY) and use it to keep your (HUD) closing statements, which you'll need to send to your clients at the end of the year. They'll need those to file for the homestead exemption (see forms #23).

7) When you purchase lockboxes, use the same code for all your boxes (this can be done at time of purchase). You must have this code in order to open the shackle on the lockboxes. It's much easier to remember one code than keep up with a different code for each lockbox. Lockboxes are the devices used to place the homeowner's keys in when you list their home. I would suggest that you purchase these as needed.

8) In case of emergencies, keep toilet paper, a flashlight, graphite (for stubborn locks), a screwdriver, pliers, and any other supplies you may need in your car.

9) Always wear your nametag. Be proud of the fact that you are a professional realtor. I have picked up numerous sales just by wearing my nametag. You never know who those people are going to be.

10) Purchase packages of note cards. Always send a note to each person you meet or speak with during the day. Don't forget to add these people to your database.

11) Prepare ten listing folders and ten buyers folders. (Look in the sellers section and buyers section of this manual for what to put in these folders).

WORKING WITH YOUR DATABASES

1) Send out a mailing to everyone in your database to introduce yourself and your new occupation. Include a magnetized business card and a regular business card. (I always tell customers the magnetized business card is so they can't lose me.) Let recipients know that you would appreciate their support for your new business. At the bottom of your letter put the tagline Your Realtor for Life. This lets people know that you mean to succeed and **succeed you will!**

2) Send newsletters each month, along with pictures and information on your current listings, sales and under contract.

3) Send quarterly information to your contacts such as how to check their credit report, community updates, and subdivision analysis, etc.

4) From your newsletter, pick an item of value (these items vary from month to month depending on the newsletter theme, it could be hand sanitizer, batteries, stamps, etc.) and visit at least three of these contacts a week. This puts you in face to face contact with your potential buyers and seller. If you're motivated to visit more than three, that's great. Send a hand-written note to everyone you visit. (see list of suggestions below). *And don't forget to ask for those referrals!*

5) Call at least three of your contacts a week. I find this easier to do after I have sent them an item of value such as my newsletter. After I contact someone, I send a hand-written note.

MARKETING AND WALKING SUBDIVISIONS[2]

1) Select a subdivision with houses in a price range that you feel comfortable working. A subdivision in which you are already selling is best. Also, make sure the subdivision has a good turnover rate.

2) Set up a file with information about the subdivision. You want to include applicable covenants, amenities, home owners association (with phone number), walking trails, streets, map, and any other information you can find to demonstrate your knowledge of the neighborhood.

3) Do a current market analysis and take it with you (have up to three folders with this information in it). Include any promotional items such as notepads, magnets, etc. I only leave these with interested parties; everyone else gets a short CMA and a business card, with my magnet attached.

---

2 D. Kennedy, *How to List and Sell Real Estate*

4) Take paper and pen to record the names, phone numbers, and addresses of anyone interested in talking with you. I carry a bag with all my information in it.

5) Walk subdivisions on Saturday between 10:00-12:00 A.M. Most people are home at that time. Always wear your nametag.

6) After knocking on a door (try not to ring the bell), step back as far as possible because you don't want to appear threatening.

7) Introduce yourself and explain your purpose. Have some fun as you meet potential clients! A possible introduction would be: Hi, I'm [your name] with [your company]. My purpose for this visit is to introduce myself. I send out postcards each month and thought you might like to meet the personality behind the face. I've sold several homes in your subdivision and would like to sell yours when the time is right. Are you looking to sell your home in the near future? If they say yes, get their name and phone number. Offer to do an extensive market analysis tailored just to their home.

8) After walking the subdivision, I send out letters (see forms #3) to the entire subdivision. I include a short market analysis to give everyone an idea of what is happening in their subdivision. I have received listings as a result of these letters. People were impressed that I had taken the time and made the effort to walk their subdivisions and introduce myself.

9) Follow-up is very important. In a month, I call every person who has given me his name and phone number, and I offer to do an extensive market analysis.

10) Continue with CMA postcard mailings in the subdivision.

11) Stay in touch with new contacts and add them to your monthly newsletter mailing list or even do a pop by (see list of suggestions below).

12) Try marketing several subdivisions at a time. If you do not get any response within six months, move on to a better subdivision. Be sure to pick a

subdivision that has a lot of sales. Again, it is easier to market a subdivision where you have already sold because people already know your name.

PERSONAL NOTES

1) Sending thank-you cards is probably one of the most important things you can do for your business. Send a thank-you note or personal note to every contact you make and do it on a daily basis. The rewards will astound you.

2) Set a goal for the number you will send out each day

3) I always send a gift certificate and a thank-you note to each person the day they send me a referral. I do not wait for the sale to close.

Sample Notes:

* It was a pleasure meeting you today. I hope we can do business in the near future.
* Just wanted to say thank-you for the referral. Referrals are the greatest compliment my customers can give me.
* Please be assured that I will take good care of your friend. A referral is a great compliment to me.
* Just a note to let you know it was a pleasure meeting you at the open house. I would enjoy working with you to find that perfect home.
* I look forward to working with you and your family on the purchase of your new home.

WEB SITE INFORMATION

1) Your own personal Web site is one of the most important tools you can create for your business.

2) A well-managed Web site can set you apart from other realtors. This is how you will receive leads for buyers as well as sellers. Make sure your keywords are potent—foreclosure listings, real estate sales, real estate, homes, properties, houses for sale, houses, property, land for sale, homes for sale, short sale, and home foreclosure.

3) You can direct your customers to your Web site, instruct them to open a pictorial tour of a current listing and tour each room in the home. On the main page, they can explore different financing options, find information about schools in the area, prequalify for a loan, and calculate what the payments on their new home would be. Also, they might be able to view numerous listings to find the new home of their dreams.

4) E-web engine (ewebengine.com) constructed and maintains my site at very little cost; they do a great job, however there are many other companies that provide this service.

IDEAS FOR VISITING PAST CUSTOMERS

You can always visit your past customers while you are on the road handling other chores. Keep your contact information handy. Always have a gift ready when you show up at their door! Check out your current month's newsletter. Sometimes it will have articles that will inspire you while preparing those gift bags. Most items that I use as gifts can be purchased at a dollar store. Get creative and use your imagination.

✓ Give a five dollar gift card for gasoline and comment that your referrals fuel my business.

✓ Give batteries for a smoke alarm and comment that I'm here to keep you safe, so when you're ready to sell your home, call on me.

✓ Sanitizing hand cleaner. I dropped by to make sure you stay germ free because I need you around to send me referrals and also to think of me when it comes time to sell your home. (Smile and make a joke of it.)

✓ Hand out one-cent stamps (buy ten) and say that I just wanted to save you the effort of going to the post office, and I also wanted to let you know that I greatly appreciate your referrals.

✓ Put together packets that highlight upcoming special events in your community and hand them out to past customers. As you hand out the packets say I like keeping informed of community events because it puts me ahead when I sell your property.

Whatever you do, always remember to

ASK FOR THOSE REFERRALS

AND HAVE FUN!

A Bit of Humor

I was fairly new to real estate and out showing houses to some potential buyers. I knocked on the door and rang the doorbell at one of my listings. No answer. Using the key from the lockbox, I unlocked the door and ushered my clients into the house. We proceeded to explore the rooms. As I opened a bedroom door, a man jumped up out of bed. He was obviously startled. So we were we. He was naked! I apologized and immediately left the house.

What more could I say?

THE ART OF
STAYING IN BUSINESS

THIS BOOK WAS WRITTEN FOR REALTORS WHO WANT TO SUCCEED AND TAKE THEIR BUSINESS TO THE NEXT LEVEL!

CUSTOMER SERVICE IS KEY TO YOUR SUCCESS

- ✓ Respect your clients; they are people too.

- ✓ Display knowledge and confidence to all your clients.

- ✓ Communication is a must; your client depends on you.

- ✓ Give each client 100 percent of your attention.

- ✓ Be sure to return all phone calls and e-mails promptly.

- ✓ Follow through and work the systems in this book.

I WISH YOU SUCCESS
ON YOUR INCREDIBLE JOURNEY!

Vicky

CHAPTER 2
WORKING WITH
SELLERS

Our success is measured only by our thoughts—not by others.

PREPARE FOR LISTING INTERVIEW

1) Conduct a comparative market analysis (CMA) and make sure you include square footage (this can be found in your tax records).

2) Obtain the tax records for your listing.

3) Print out the past year's sales in subdivision on a spreadsheet like Excel. You can do this in the tax record section of your listing service. This gives you all the sales, including those by owners, and the square footage for each home.

4) Create a seller net sheet. Prepare three scenarios using different price ranges.

5) Create a listing package as described in this section.

6) Prepare an exclusive sellers listing agreement that is dated to be effective for six months and filled out except for the listing dates.

7) E-mail the seller the property disclosure (if possible), so he can fill this out in advance. I use this approach with customers I already know.

8) For new listing appointments, drop off your listing presentation packet. This gives you an opportunity to meet the seller if you've only spoken on the phone. Be sure to take a picture of the front of the home to use on your CMA. Your packet should include your resume, several letters of recommendations, web site information, copy of one of your flyers, staging information and a property disclosure. Also, be sure to ask the seller to have the following ready for you:
   a) Security deed for legal description
   b) Home owners association information (see forms #4)
   c) Copy of their plat
   d) Copy of their covenants and restrictions.
   e) Utility information

9) Take a lockbox, Sale sign, and camera.

10) Take pictures of the front, back, and interior of the house.

11) Be careful to explain to your seller how the lockbox works and to find out if there are times that need to be blocked out for showings.

12) **Always** send a **thank-you note** after the initial appointment.

A Bit of Humor

Once I had a seller call my broker to let him know I did not deserve my commission because I hung the phone up on him at 1:00 A.M.! Yes, 1:00 in the morning. My broker replied that he had been paid the commission and would give it to whomever he chose!!

LISTING FOLDERS

These folders should include the following items:

1. Your magnetized business card plus a regular business card

2. Home warranty information (Old Republic offers six months limited coverage free to the seller.)

3. Your Web site advertising information (see forms #5)

4. Recommended termite control companies (at least three)

5. Recommended home inspection companies (at least three); (Some companies conduct prelisting inspections.)

6. Exclusive seller listing agreement (two copies, filled out except for the listing period)

7. Seller's property disclosure statement

8. Association/Assessment fee exhibit

9. Data entry input sheet

10. Homeowners Association (HOA) subdivision information sheet (See forms #4)

11. Comparative Market Analysis (CMA)

12. Net sheet that includes three different pricing scenarios

13. Top ten rules for staging (see forms #6)

14. Utility company information sheet

15. Your marketing plan (see forms #7)

16. Exit guarantee (see forms #8)

ABOVE ALL BE PREPARED. SHOW YOUR SELLER THAT YOU HAVE ALL THE INFORMATION and EXPERTISE NEEDED TO MAKE THEIR SELLING EXPERIENCE POSITIVE AND STRESS FREE

THIS IS A BUSINESS!
RUN IT LIKE ONE!

POST LISTING PROCEDURES

1) Fill in all information on your listing information sheet and turn into office within twenty-four hours (see forms #19)

2) Upload pictures of the house, downsize and place on your Web site, listing service, etc.

3) Prepare a custom flyer

   a) Start with fifty black-and-white flyers; then print color (The neighbors usually take the first ones.)
   b) If the home has a lot of features, create a page listing the special features and place it on the back of the flyer.

4) Put together a notebook that includes information on schools, covenants, the subdivision, plat, and the property disclosure. Include anything that pertains to the home and community.

5) Print just-listed postcards and mail to residents of the subdivision.

6) Create CDs with all your interior pictures. Deliver CDs, notebook, and flyers to the property.

7) Order a home warranty if applicable.

8) Order a termite letter if the seller gives his okay. I like to ensure there isn't a termite problem.

9) Be sure to reference you listing number to your lockbox.

10) Review property disclosure and upload to your listing service.

11) Review your listing information on your listing service for accuracy.

12) In the first week send Web pictures and a copy of listings to the seller. (Always make sure your seller has a copy of everything he has signed.)

13) Call the seller with weekly showings and any feedback.

MAKE YOUR SELLERS PROUD THAT THEY HIRED YOU FOR THE JOB!

STAY IN TOUCH!

THE CONTRACT AND SETTING UP THE CLOSING (See Forms #21)

1) Turn the fully executed sales contract, contract processing sheet (see forms #11), and the commission agreement into your office.

2) A fully executed contract is a contract that has been signed, initialed and agreed upon by all parties.

3) If your purchaser the amendment to remove the inspection contingency is your next concern.

   a. Have purchaser set up all appointments, i.e., home inspector, termite inspector, pool inspector, any and all due diligence item.
   b. Ensure you know the time frame within which all inspections must be completed.

4) Fax a copy of the contract and any changes to closing attorney. Set up appointment time for the closing and obtain directions to the closing attorney.

5) Inform the other agent and your seller of the closing time and date.

6) Purchase a gift if your purchaser. I enjoy giving live plants and arrangements.

7) Send directions and utility information to the purchaser's agent.

8) Call your seller to remind him to bring his drivers license, any receipts for repairs, keys, and garage door openers.

9) Call in the home warranty if applicable. Be sure to print a copy of the receipt to give to the purchaser at the closing along with a copy of the warranty plan. You can usually get this at your office.

10) On the day of the closing remove the real estate sign, lockbox, and listing book.

11) Always attend the closing and review the HUD statement (attorneys closing statement) for accuracy.

REMEMBER, YOU ARE REPRESENTING YOUR SELLER; HE NEEDS YOU TO BE THERE FOR HIM. YOU ARE MORE LIKELY TO RECEIVE REFERRALS IF YOU DO YOUR JOB!

CHAPTER 3
WORKING WITH
BUYERS

Remember, we are what we think we are—not what others think of us.

BUYERS

1) Buyers can be a lot of fun if you are prepared for them.

2) Gather information by using the buyer information record sheet (see forms #10)

3) Once you have all their specifications, e-mail all suitable listings to them and allow them to choose what they want to see. Try to stick to ten showings at a time; after the tenth showing, everything runs together.

4) Call each seller to schedule an approximate time for the showing, if they do not answer, leave a message with your approximate arrival time and call the realtor to make sure the property is still available.

5) Route each property. (You will need to look at your directions on each listing and determine the best route and order to show.)

6) When showing properties, always knock and ring the doorbell before using a key to enter. You never know what surprises lurk on the other side of that door. Be respectful of others' property by turning off lights and making sure all doors are locked when you leave.

7) Meet, show, and have fun.

8) **Never allow a potential buyer to leave your car without first scheduling the next appointment.**

9) Send a thank-you note.

10) Immediately add the buyer to your monthly mailing list.

A Bit of Humor

I spent at least ten months showing houses to one couple. By the third month, we'd gotten to know each other pretty well—the husband even named my navigational system for me. It became known as "Miss Di" because of all the misdirection's she gave us. When I finally found them a home they loved, I told the husband that I sure was going to miss our Sunday dates! He and his wife laughed!

BUYERS FOLDERS

These folders should include:

1. Recommended lender information

2. Your business card and your magnetized business card

3. Information on various types of loans, including FHA and VA

4. A map because most buyers are looking in new areas or towns.

5. Home warranty information

6. Recommended termite companies

7. Recommended inspection companies

8. CMA buyers' information—even tax records sometimes—on each subdivision you are showing

9. Community and school information

10. Purchase and sale agreement (2 copies)

11. Buyer's brokerage agreement (2 copies)

12. Financing contingency form (2 copies)

13. FHA loan exhibit (2 copies)

14. Appraisal contingency exhibit (2 copies)

15. Association/Assessment fee exhibit (2 copies)

16. Your Web site information (see forms #5)

17. Commission agreement

18. Moving with children information (see forms #12)

ABOVE ALL, BE PREPARED. SHOW YOUR BUYER THAT YOU HAVE ALL THE INFORMATION and EXPERTISE NEEDED TO MAKE HIS BUYING EXPERIENCE POSITIVE AND STRESS FREE.

WHY BUYERS SHOULD USE AN AGENT

What are the pitfalls of going it alone?

✓ Without a real estate professional, the buyer may not have access to all the information he needs to make a knowledgeable buying decision. Without a comparative market analysis, he could be paying more for a home than it's worth.

✓ The buyer may be buying a money pit. The property could have major problems that aren't reflected in the listing price, and maybe the owner could not get a real estate professional to list their property. Most real estate professionals won't waste their time trying to market a home that has no reasonable chance of selling.

✓ If you have deadlines for selling your current home or need to relocate because of a job change, a real estate professional can help move things along.

Then there's that new home subdivision

✓ The subdivision agent is looking out for the interests of the seller/builder.

✓ How do you know you are getting the best price possible? Without a CMA, you could be paying more for a home than it's worth.

✓ How do you know what the other homes in the subdivision have sold for? Your realtor will do the homework for you.

✓ With a realtor on your side, you are protected and receive all the facts from a professional. Also, at closing, you have someone there to protect your interest.[3]

---

3 source ewebengine.com

A Bit of Humor

I went to a closing for one of my customers who purchased a home from a subdivision agent (without me). At the closing, they tried to cheat him out of the closing cost the builder was supposed to pay. Not knowing how to read the Hud statement, he would have never known. The builder actually tried to have me removed from the closing. The closing attorney tore up the first closing statement and produced a correct one after I called them on what they termed an *error*!

VERY IMPORTANT

Before the due diligence period expires, you should have all the following, if applicable, completed.

✓ Survey—make sure the home and any fences are within the property lines

✓ Loan—make sure your customer is approved through underwriting

✓ Floodplain-make sure the house isn't on a floodplain (the lender should check this)

✓ Inspection—make sure all inspections (home, termite, pool, roof, septic, survey, etc.) are done

✓ Appraisal—make sure the home's appraisal meets the contract price (the lender should check this)

✓ Lead Paint—make sure the house has been checked for lead paint, and if it's present, make sure all disclosures are signed

*Due Diligence rules may vary from state to state so please check with your local board or real estate organization for your state's specific rules.

IF YOUR CUSTOMER DECIDES TO BACK OUT, FOR ANY OF THE REASONS GIVEN ABOVE, AFTER THE DUE DILIGENCE PERIOD EXPIRES, HIS EARNEST MONEY IS

NON-REFUNDABLE!

AFTER THE SALE

1) See page 21 of this manual "the contract and setting up the closing" and follow these procedures to facilitate a smooth closing.

2) Be sure to stay in touch with your purchaser. Give them up-to-date information on the closing and be there to answer their questions.

3) Take pictures of the inside and outside of the purchaser's new home and copy to multiple CD's. They will appreciate your extra effort and will be pleased to receive them as they are great to send to friends and family.

4) Print address labels with their new address. These make a nice gift at closing.

5) The closing attorney will send a form that requires the purchaser's information. Forward this to the purchaser and ask them to fax or e-mail the form directly to the closing attorney. This way you are not responsible for their personal information. *i.e.* social security number.

6) Contact the closing attorney several days before closing to make sure they have the closing package. If the package is not there this will alert you in advance there may be a potential problem. The next step is to contact the lender to inquire about the progress of the loan and the closing date.

7) Ask the closing attorney to e-mail you the HUD statement. In the beginning, ask the attorney's office and your broker to help you understand this document. The HUD statement will tell the purchaser the amount of funds they need to bring to closing. Also, these funds must be a certified check made payable to you the purchaser. In some instances the funds can be wired to the attorney's office before closing. (These instructions may vary from state to state.)

8) Be sure to fill out the anniversary tract sheet (see forms #1) and place in appropriate month for next year's follow-up and CMA. Add purchaser to your monthly mailing list and send post closing letter in two weeks. (see forms #9)

**ALWAYS ATTEND THE CLOSING.
REMEMBER, YOU ARE REPRESENTING YOUR BUYER; HE NEEDS
YOU TO BE THERE FOR HIM. YOU ARE MORE LIKELY TO RECEIVE
REFERRALS IF YOU DO YOUR JOB!**

CHAPTER 4 WORKING WITH FOR-SALE-BY-OWNERS

Choose Courage Not Fear

FOR-SALE-BY-OWNER PROCEDURES

Place the following items in a folder:

a) A copy of introducing contract/closing services for sale by owners letter *(see forms #13)*

b) A copy of purchase and sale agreement and the property disclosure statement; include a handwritten note along the lines of: Sorry you're leaving us! Here are copies of the forms you'll need to sell your home. If you'd like an explanation of any of the terms, please give me a call. No obligation. Sincerely, [your name]

c) Your provider list

a) Seller's net sheet

b) Subdivision CMA(Comparative Market Analysis)

c) Marketing plan (see forms #7)

d) Sign-in sheet for their prospective buyers; ask the seller if you can have this information for your personal use. *(see forms #14)*

e) Include your business card and a magnetized business card

1) Be willing to do an open house, but be sure you have the seller complete a permission to show unlisted property form before the open house. If you provide the buyer, you will need to reach an agreement about your commission with the seller.

2) If possible, inform the seller that you could offer free marketing of his house on your Web site.

3) Be sure to take a camera to take pictures and create a flyer for the seller.

WORK SMARTER NOT HARDER!

A Bit of Humor

Once I contacted a couple who had chosen the for-sale-by-owner route and asked
if I could hold their house open while I also held an open house for one of my
listings. They loved the idea. I sold their house that day! The owner of my listing
was so upset that I didn't sell his house that day he fired me!

TRY THIS; IT WORK'S

***About two weeks before you hold an open house, visit all for sale by owners in that subdivision. Explain to them you are holding an open house at your listing in their subdivision and would like to include their home.

Explain that they would set a price and agree to pay you a (TBD) percent commission in the event their home sells. They would sign an agreement to show unlisted property. If the seller allows you to preview the home, note all pertinent details needed to market the sale and complete a disclosure statement. Take pictures, prepare flyers, and have fun.

THE GOOD NEWS IS THAT EVEN IF THE PROPERTY DOES NOT SELL, YOU WILL USUALLY GET THE LISTING!

CHAPTER 5
HOLDING AN
OPEN HOUSE

Persistence paves the way to success

AN EFFECTIVE OPEN HOUSE

How to set the stage for an open house:

1) Make a sign that reads Welcome to My Open House and sign your name at bottom. Place this on the kitchen counter along with your flyers.

2) Run ad in the local paper. Also put the open house ad in your multiple listing services.

3) Mail postcards announcing the open house to friends, coworkers, and neighbors.

4) Place open house signs in advance—preferably on Wednesday if you are holding your house open on Sunday.

5) Distribute handouts or door hangers in surrounding neighborhoods where houses are in a lower price range. If management allows, also distribute them at nearby apartments, duplexes and short-stay hotels with out-of-town residents.

6) Call and invite all neighbors and ask that they bring a friend. You can say something like:

> I am calling to let you know I am having an open house at [address here]_____ at one o'clock this Sunday. There will be refreshments, and I would like to invite you and a friend to drop by. Do you think you might have time to drop by? If the answer is *yes*, send the person a reminder and a thank-you note.

7) Hold an open house on Sunday from 2:00 to 5:00 or 1:00 to 4:00. The sellers must not be present during the open house.

8) Have a current market analysis available for potential buyers.

9) Have a please sign-in sheet available (see forms #14).

10) Have a contract filled out complete with legal description of the property and be sure to bring a pen and calculator.

11) Play music in the background.

12) Make up a list of exceptional features to go with flyer and to hand out to buyers.

13) Make signs using brightly colored paper to show the home's outstanding features:

> Time-Saving, Built-In Microwave
> Spacious Master Bedroom
> Sparkling Pool
> Oak Hardwood Floors
> What a View
> Cozy Fireplace
> Extra Insulation
> Granite Countertops

14) Bring the following items with you:

> Open House Signs for the front of the home and all corners
> Directionals
> Balloons to attach to the signs
> Open Come In sign
> Coffee, creamer, and sugar
> Soft drinks and water
> Styrofoam cups
> Cookies (Bake these) (be sure to ask the owner's permission)
> Vanilla extract (place a few drops on a cookie sheet and put in the oven on low heat) (Do this if you are not baking cookies and be sure to ask the owner's permission)
> Flame logs (2) (only in winter) (be sure to ask the owner's permission)

15) Before the open house, give your sellers a copy of the top ten rules for staging your home (see forms #6). This will set the stage for a professional open house.

16) Check out the for-sale-by-owner information given on page 39, use your initiative and contact those for sale by owners!

MEET, GREET, AND HAVE FUN!

A Bit of Humor

I once hired an agent and thought to myself, "Great! Now I won't have to do open houses any more!" Wrong! My seller called to let me know that the agent had three, yes, three buyers (it was an $800,000 listing). When the seller asked the agent to call the prospective buyers and get some feedback, the agent replied that she couldn't take down the telephone numbers because she had forgotten to bring a pen! Forgotten to bring a pen? Needless to say I lost that listing.

CHAPTER 6
WORKING A LEASE
PURCHASE SALE

Your state of mind is very important when creating a new career

WHAT IS A LEASE PURCHASE?

1) What is a lease purchase?
   A lease purchase agreement is a contract whereby the seller agrees that the buyer has the option of buying the property at the end of the lease period. The security deposit is nonrefundable. Usually, some or all of the deposit and payments made under the lease are applied to the purchase price if, at the end of the lease, the buyer should decide to exercise the option to purchase the property.

2) Why use lease purchase instead of buying?
   Many people are unable to obtain financing for the purchase of a home. A lease purchase agreement permits people with less than perfect credit or those with little money available for a down payment to purchase a home. It gives the purchaser a year or two to get his credit in order.

3) What are the advantages of a lease purchase?
   Even though the property value is increasing every year the purchase price is set.

4) What are the disadvantages of a lease purchase? The purchaser would not receive the advantage of a tax deduction for the interest on the house payments. Also, since he is paying the seller directly, he risks the seller going bankrupt or losing the property to foreclosure, which would preclude his purchase of the house.

5) Title to the property remains with the seller until the buyer exercises the purchase agreement.

A Bit of Humor

One of the first things I learned the hard way was to never tell a customer he has an offer or someone is interested in his property. Often, the offer does not come through, and you have to eat a lot of crow!!

Learning the unknown will bring great rewards

PREPARING A LEASE PURCHASE CONTRACT

1) You will need the following forms:
   a. Lease purchase agreement (requires a nonrefundable security deposit)
   b. Lease for lease purchase agreement (requires one month's rent as a deposit)
   c. Seller's property disclosure statement
   d. Owner's property disclosure statement (lease)
   e. Exclusive buyer brokerage agreement (if you're representing the tenant-buyer)
   f. Move-in/move-out inspection form
   g. Pet exhibit (if applicable)
   h. Lead-based paint exhibit (if applicable)

2) You must remember this involves two contracts—one for the lease and one for the lease purchase. You will need a security deposit for the lease agreement and earnest money for the lease-purchase agreement. The landlord-seller or your real estate broker can hold the security deposit.

3) The due diligence period and all other contingency periods should begin and end before the tenant-buyer takes possession. This would mean that if the buyer-tenant fails to close according to the contract, the earnest money would go to the landlord-seller (unless the landlord-seller defaults).

4) It is important for the landlord-seller to walk through the property with the tenant-buyer and fill out the move-in/move-out inspection form. This must be done before the tenant-buyer takes possession of the property. This records the condition of the property at move-in time and makes dealing with the security deposit later much easier.

5) If possible, the agents should get the month's rent deposit as a commission as these lease-purchase deals don't have a good track record for closing.

6) If part of the rent is being credited back to the tenant-buyer at closing, that part cannot exceed the amount of rent collected above fair rental value. For example, if fair rental value is $1,000, and the rent collected is $1,500, only $500 can be credited back to the tenant-buyer. You must clear this with the lender (underwriter).

7) It is very important to get the tenant-buyer prequalified before the landlord-seller signs these contracts (see forms #24 and #25). Also, I recommend that you place these buyers with a lender who can help them repair their credit and keep you apprised of the situation. You want to give them every opportunity to be able to close at the end of their lease. [4]

A Bit of Humor

I met with a seller to discuss listing her home. After she got through complaining about all the past agents she had, I told her I did not want the listing! She was incredulous and asked, "Why not?"

---

[4] Unknown source

CHAPTER 7 WORKING A SHORT SALE PLUS HUD FORECLOSURE INFORMATION

Whenever we help another, we also help ourselves

WHAT ARE HUD HOMES?

1) HUD (Housing and Urban Development) homes are homes that have been lost to foreclosure.

2) Any licensed real estate professional is eligible to sell HUD homes.

3) In order to qualify to sell HUD homes, your designated broker must complete the required forms and receive a NAID (Name and Address Identifier Number) number from PEMCO, Ltd.

4) Once your employing broker becomes certified, you may show, advertise, and submit bids on HUD homes.

5) I recommend that you take a class (visit www.hudpemco.com for locations and dates). A HUD key will be issued at that time or you can use your managing broker's key. This key will allow you to enter all HUD foreclosed homes. These homes are not on regular lockboxes. You will receive instructions on how to submit a contract, how to advertise HUD homes, and what is required when you take your class.

6) The sales contract is filled out online at www.hudpemco.com. Complete instructions are available on the Web site.

WHAT IS A SHORT SALE?

1) A short sale is a bank-owned property on which the lender is willing to accept considerably less than is owed. The owner generally still holds title and will continue to do so until the sale is complete. The lender gets the proceeds of the sale and discharges the remaining debt. The home owner must leave the house as soon as it is sold (closed).

2) According to sources in the mortgage industry, people who agree to a short sale with the lender do far less damage to their credit rating than those who go through foreclosure. Some lenders will issue a 1099 form at closing for the difference between what is owed the bank and what was realized from the sale. Check with the lenders as to how this affects the sellers, if any.

3) A foreclosure occurs when borrowers have not made two or more mortgage payments, and the lenders respond by filing a legal notice and commencing a legal proceeding to take possession of the home.

SHORT-SALE PROCEDURES

1) The first thing you must learn is to listen!

2) Listen for the clues and ask questions. Tell your seller that if he ever gets in a situation where he is behind on his mortgage, to please let you know. There is help. Rather he/she chooses to do a modification or a short sale, in most cases there is another solution.

3) The seller needs to be at least thirty days behind in his mortgage payments before you can start a short-sale procedure.

4) Most lenders want an offer before they will proceed but not all. When you call the lender to get the payoff amount, you can ask about this.

5) Have your seller fill out an authorization form (see forms #15). Then you will call the lender and ask for loss mitigation; the lender will provide a fax number to which you will send the completed form. About two days later, the lender will be able to discuss the case with you. Then you will find out if the lender is willing to do a short sale and, if so, you'll receive the payoff information that you will need to proceed. Once you know the payoff, you can reduce the price of your listing. Most homes are marked down at least 20 percent, but you must ensure that your commission will be covered after the markdown.

In other words, only reduce the price by whatever you have agreed upon your commission to be, subtract that from the 20 percent. Because the lender doesn't have to accept the reduced price, make sure you have a disclosure on the listing that reads: All terms, offers, and conditions are subject to seller's lender's approval. Please call agent for a copy of special stipulations.

6) Next, have your seller get together all the information that is requested on the short sale checklist (see forms # 16).

7) Make sure you prepare an amendment to send to all potential offers that includes the following (see forms #17):

SPECIAL STIPULATIONS

1) Buyer acknowledges that the sale of the property will not generate sufficient cash to pay off the mortgage(s) on the property and the other obligations of seller with respect to this purchase and sale transaction. This agreement is therefore contingent upon seller's mortgage lenders(s) agreeing to: (1) take a reduced payoff on its mortgage(s) in an amount sufficient such that the purchase price of the property pays off the reduced amount of the mortgage(s), any other liens, judgments, and other encumbrances on the property, the real estate commission(s) owing to the broker(s), and the other expenses of sale for which seller is obligated under this agreement without seller having to pay any additional sums: and (2) release seller from any claim, cause of action, suit or judgment for the amount of the reduction in the payoff on said mortgage(s). In the event, the mortgage lender(s) do not agree to such reduction at least ten days before closing, either seller or buyer may terminate this agreement without penalty upon written notice to the other party.[5]

2) Buyers and sellers acknowledge that all terms, offers, and conditions are subject to approval by the seller's lender(s).

---

5 Source GA Assoc. of Realtors SS 516 , Short Sale Contingency, copyright 2009

3) Buyers and sellers acknowledge that property is being sold *as is*, with no repairs.

4) All short-sale closings are to be held at (**Here you can enter your closing attorney's information, but check first to make sure he handles short sales)**

5) Acceptance date will be when the seller's lender(s) accepts the contract. All due diligence will start at that time.

8) Once you have an offer and the seller has signed off on the contract, it can be sent (put the loan number on each page) to the lender with a net sheet (see forms #18). You can call the closing attorney and ask him to run a tax information sheet for any past-due taxes or other outstanding liens. Once the forms have been sent, you should receive a call from the lender within five days. At that time, you will be assigned a loss mitigation person. If you don't receive that call, you should call the lender.

9) Be aware that most lenders will not pay for home warranties, termite letters, or closing costs. I always explain this to the purchaser's agent up front. Also, it is my experience that all short sales are sold *as is*.

10) Most lenders take a while to get you an answer regarding approval of the offer for the house. It's best to make the buyer aware that this is not a quick process and ask for his patience. It can take up to six weeks. In my experience, the wait is typically four weeks, but you must stay in touch with your loss mitigation person. Also, don't be shy about asking for that person's supervisor. I have had to do this a few times. Communication is very important.

Working with short sales contracts can be a very rewarding experience because your purchaser will receive an excellent deal on a property and your seller will not be stuck with a foreclosure on their credit.

There are situations in which the lender will allow other remedies:

✓ Sign the title over to the bank (Deed in Lieu of Foreclosure)

✓ Some lenders will pay a fee to leave the home in excellent condition.

✓ Some lenders will do a modification that can include, reducing the interest rate and extending the mortgage from thirty to forty years.

✓ Some lenders will renegotiate to modify an existing loan or request forbearance.

Have the seller visit his lender's Web site, look for information on loss mitigation, and speak to a representation about his situation. You won't make any money off these sales, but these people will never forget you and will recommend you to all their friends and relatives.

A Bit of Humor

I had a contract on a short sale, but the seller moved out unexpectedly,
and I couldn't find him. So much for all that work.
Oh, well!!

CHAPTER 8
FORMS

FORMS LIST

1) Anniversary Track Sheet
2) Request Your Free Credit Report Today - Letter
3) Hi Neighbors- Subdivision Letter
4) Home Owners Association Form
5) Web Site/Marketing Information Example
6) Rules of Staging
7) Marketing Plan
8) Exit Guarantee
9) Post Closing Letter
10) Buyer Information Sheet
11) Contract Processing Form
12) Moving with Children
13) For-Sale-By-Owner Letter
14) Sign in Sheet
15) Short Sale Authorization Letter
16) Short Sale Checklist
17) Short Sale Special Stipulations
18) Short Sale Net Sheet
19) Listing Information Sheet
20) Offer Work Sheet
21) Setting up the Closing
22) Anniversary Letter
23) Letter for Filing Homestead Exemption
24) Authorization for Credit Check
25) Rental Application

*SEE PAGE 95 TO ORDER CUSTOMIZABLE FORMS ON CD

#1   **ANNIVERSARY TRACK SHEET**

Name _____

Address _____

Date of Closing _____

Subdivision _____

Original Purchase Price _____

Children's Names _____

Telephone Numbers
Home _____
Cell _____
Work _____
Fax _____
E-Mail _____

Get information from HUD (closing statement)
Attach all flyers and computer print outs
Enter information on agent office or contact management software
Send: Original purchase price
**   Estimate of current market value**
**   One-year anniversary letter**

- **Make a file January – December**
- **Place this form in appropriate month of closing**
- **Pull form each month and send CMA and letter**

#2

Logo
**Company
Name
Contact Information
Web Site**

Request Your Free Credit Report Today!

You are entitled to receive one free credit report from each of the nationwide consumer-credit reporting companies every twelve months. You can request your credit score by contacting one of the agencies listed below.

Your can make you request by mail or on their Web site:

Equifax
1-877-576-5734   www.equifax.com
P.O. Box 740256
Atlanta, Ga 30374

Experian
1-888-397-3742   www.experian.com
P.O. Box 9532
Allen, Texas 75013

TransUnion
1-800-680-7289   www.transunion.com
P.O. Box 6790
Fullerton, CA 92834

*Call them in advance to obtain the list of information they need to process a request made through their Web site.

Sincerely,

Your Name
Realtor

If any of your friends or relatives are thinking about buying or selling a home, I'd love to be of service to them. So, when you think of these people, just give me a call with their names and business numbers. I'll be happy to follow up and meet their real estate needs.

"If the property is currently listed, please disregard this letter. It is not our intention to solicit another broker's listing."

#3

Logo
**Company
Name
Contact Information
Web Site**

Date

Hi, Neighbors,

Last Saturday I had the opportunity to meet many residents as I walked through [Subdivision Name] and introduced myself. Meeting you has provided me with the chance to get to know your community better and to gather information about schools and amenities that will enable me to extend the best service possible. Hopefully, I will soon be able to meet those of you that I missed.

[**Subdivision Name**] is a beautiful community, and representing you in any real estate transaction would be a pleasure. Please give me a call when you find yourself in need of a real estate professional that specializes in your area.

Enclosed is a copy of a newsletter with information on the just-listed, and recently sold homes in [**Subdivision Name**]. This information will provide an ideal as to your current market status. However, I would be happy to prepare a free market analysis that is customized to your home; it will give you a better idea of your home's value.

Please visit my Web site [provide URL here] and explore what is one of my most powerful listing tools. There you can open a pictorial tour of a current listing and tour each room in the home. On my main Web page, you can explore different financing options, find information on schools in the area, prequalify for a loan, and calculate the payments on your new home. With just one stop, you can view numerous listings.

I welcome your phone call and the opportunity to be of service to you. Thank you for your time.

Sincerely,

Signature
[typed name]

"If the property is currently listed, please disregard this letter. It is not our intention to solicit another broker's listing."

#4   **HOME OWNERS ASSOCIATION FORM**

HOA INFORMATION

Property Address: _____

Subdivision Name: _____

HOA Contact Name: _____

HOA Contact Phone: _____

#5   *Example*

WEB SITE/MARKETING INFORMATION

WWW.EXCEPTIONALREALTORSGROUP.COM

WWW.EXCEPTIONALMOUNTAINLIVING.COM

WWW.*Your Name*.COM

WWW.REALTOR.COM

WWW.FMLS.COM

WWW.GAMLS.COM

WWW.ATLANTAMLS.COM

EXCEPTIONALREALTORSGROUP.GEORGIAMLS.COM

EXAMINER.COM

USNETADS.COM

BACKPAGE.COM

HGTV (FRONTDOOR.COM)

CLRSEARCH.COM

LAKEHOMESUSA.COM

HOTPADS.COM

MYREALTY.COM

ZILLOW.COM

WALMART.OODLE.COM

LAKEHOMESUSA.COM

PROPERTYQUBE.COM

OPENHOUSE.COM

ALSO, LISTED ON OODLE, GOOGLE BASE, GEEBO, TRULIA, PROPSMART, EDGEIO, LYCOS, REAL ESTATE BULLETIN BOARD, VAST, OLX, CYBERHOMES, HOMESCAPE, YAHOO CLASSIFIED, PROPBOT, and AOL REAL ESTATE

#6   Rules of Staging [6]

1. Curb Appeal!

You've seen them—"buyers who drive slowly by your house judging its appearance and deciding whether to request a showing or attend an open house". Make these potential buyers fall in love with your house at first glance by adding potted plants and flowers, power-washing patios and walkways, weeding the garden, and mowing the lawn. It's your first chance to make a good impression, so you've got to make it count!

2. Remove the Odors!

Pay particular attention to odors. You might even consider having a friend drop by for a smell test. Odors— especially **pet odors—**are **the number one reason a home does not sell. The number two reason is the odor of cigarette smoke!**

3. Open Your Blinds and Have Someone Be Honest about Your Colors!

Neutralize strong colors for the broadest appeal. A neutral home appears larger and is less likely to offend someone. Also, open blinds and draperies, so there is sufficient light throughout the home. Remember, lighting is the most effective way to set a mood.

4. Depersonalize!

Few things deter buyers more than clutter. They need to see your home not your stuff. Excessive personal items like photos, collections, personal awards, electronics, and collectibles will make it difficult for buyers to see past your personal style and may prevent a sale. Taking yourself out of the picture makes it easier for buyers to imagine themselves and their stuff in your space.

5. Professional Stager!

Think about removing or replacing worn out or outdated furnishings. Get rid of extra pieces of furniture. The time has come to move beyond matching furniture, so break up your sets. Consider consulting a **professional staging company** for design direction and advice on using **rental furnishings** to create an inviting home that will appeal to a wide range of buyers.

---

6 Top 10 rules of staging from the stagers, www.hgtv.com, 2008

6. Lighting!

Renew the look of a room by replacing old or dated light fixtures, door hardware, light switches, and outlets. If it's tacky and older than you, get it out of there!

7. Artwork!

Displaying new artwork is a great way to breathe new life into a room. Photography can be used to contemporize a room and add a pop of color as well. Be sure to remove any art that includes nudity because it can offend some buyers.

8. Make repairs!

Make your home a well maintained zone. Fix squeaky doors, chipped or smudged paint, and broken fixtures and fittings that you've neglected.

9. Apply a Fresh Coat of Paint!

It's the best bang for your buck when you want to quickly refresh a dull, dated room. Slap a fresh, neutral color on the space. Choose beige or taupe for living spaces and a neutral green or blue for bathrooms.

10. Don't Forget the Floors!

Get rid of worn carpets and consider refinishing shabby hardwood floors. A new inexpensive area rug is a quick fix and can disguise the look of old floors.

CHECKLIST FOR FASTER SALES

First impressions are lasting, and you don't get a second chance to make a good one. Most buyers are looking for a house that's clean, spiffy, and brightly lit. Ensuring that your house is immaculate and properly maintained will do more than anything else to make a potential buyer determined to find a way to buy. This checklist covers those items that are most likely to positively influence a buyer.

OUTSIDE:

- ✓ Sweep driveways and sidewalks; keep them free of toys, bicycles, garden hoses, and other hazards. Fill potholes in driveways and walkways (you can buy concrete in a tube for this).
- ✓ Clean twigs and leaves from gutters and sweep roof. If gutters sag, straighten or replace.
- ✓ Wash windows, screens, and all glass doors.
- ✓ Paint, fix, or wash railings and steps.
- ✓ Very important—brighten the front door with a fresh coat of paint or stain, or a good cleaning.   Remove any mold or mildew from home and walkways.
- ✓ Polish front doorknob, knocker, and kickplate. If they're badly tarnished, replace them.
- ✓ Replace burned-out bulbs in outside fixtures and polish or clean the fixtures.
- ✓ If necessary, paint the house's exterior or pressure wash vinyl siding.
- ✓ Rid the driveway and/or garage or carport of grease stains. You can use kitty litter or a chemical solvent to do this.
- ✓ Tidy garage and make it appear as big as it really is. Get rid of everything you don't want to move. A garage sale might be a good idea.
- ✓ Clean air conditioner or compressor.
- ✓ Roll out the welcome mat with a rough-textured doormat. It will help keep your floors clean during showings, and it says that you care about your home.
- ✓ Clean all outdoor furniture and remove rust stains.
- ✓ Fix doorbells, tighten loose doorknobs, spray silicone or WD 40 in locks, oil squeaky hinges, and adjust doors that don't lock easily.

INSIDE:

- ✓ Perk up a room with paint. Choose neutral colors.
- ✓ Keep the kitchen especially clean. This is a very important room to women prospects. Clear counters of excess clutter but don't leave them empty. Mop and wax floors and put away dirty dishes. Clean stove, refrigerator, and sink. Clean out cupboards and pantry. Take almost all magnets off the refrigerator. Clean and degrease the oven.

- ✓ Keep you bathroom clean. To improve its appearance, replace caulking or grout. Replace washers in dripping faucets and fix leaky toilets. Matching towels will improve the appearance.
- ✓ Eliminate odors by preventing them in the first place. Avoid cooking with cabbage, onions, or garlic. Many folks associate strong, spicy odors with uncleanliness. Freshen up the kitchen by sending a lemon through the garbage disposal. Place decorative air fresheners in front of heat/AC vents or use plug-in air fresheners (vanilla scent). Carpets should be cleaned or replaced if badly worn or stained. Use a deodorizer in the cleaning solution. A carpet allowance may be an alternative, but since most buyers are visual, replace if possible.
- ✓ Vacuum or dust blinds and windowsills. Remove worn curtains.
- ✓ Clear out and organize closets to make them appear roomier. Pack out of season clothing and donate clothes you no longer wear to charity.
- ✓ Clear clutter from attic, basement, or storage areas. This allows the buyer to see the potential of these areas.
- ✓ Lubricate sticking doors, windows, and drawers with candle wax. Tighten loose doorknobs and faucets, and oil hinges.
- ✓ Make beds.
- ✓ Remove some pieces of furniture from crowded rooms to increase the feeling of spaciousness. The furniture can be stored or donated to charity.
- ✓ Remove personal items like posters, signs, personal artwork (especially any with nudity) and personal photos.

HOW TO HELP SALES AGENTS:

- ✓ Children, pets, and adults can keep buyers from feeling at ease and make them hurry through the house. For showings, please be out of the house if possible.
- ✓ Try to keep pets restrained during the day while you are away, so buyers won't feel nervous.
- ✓ Turn television or stereo down or off during showings. Sight and sound distractions can kill a buyer's interest.
- ✓ When at home, leave the showing to the salesperson. He/she knows the buyer's requirements and can best emphasize the features of your house

that are important to that particular buyer. You will be called if needed. Never volunteer information that is not requested.

✓ Don't discuss anything concerning the sale with the buyer. Let the salesperson discuss price, terms, possession, and other factors with the buyer. He/she is eminently qualified to bring negotiations to a favorable conclusion.

Expending a little extra energy can go a long way toward enhancing your home. Look at it as an investment in your property.

#7   MY COMMITMENT TO YOU

- ✓ AM ACCOUNTABLE.
- ✓ YOU WILL SEE THE RESULTS.
- ✓ WE WILL WORK TOGETHER TO SELL YOUR HOME AT THE BEST PRICE AND TERMS POSSIBLE.
- ✓ I WILL ENSURE THAT YOUR PROPERTY IS FULLY EXPOSED IN THE MARKET AS QUICKLY AS POSSIBLE.
- ✓ I WILL MAINTAIN GOOD COMMUNICATION WITH YOU.

MARKETING PLAN

1. In-depth consultation with the seller.
2. Fill our all paperwork accurately and take pictures.
3. Install for sale sign and lock box.
4. Design custom property brochure.
5. Design special feature list.
6. Review showing procedure and explain how lockbox works.
7. Advise seller to obtain loan payoff.
8. Submit listing to company and personal Web site.
9. Submit to multiple listing services.
10. Discuss and schedule open house.
11. Present all offers to you and help you obtain the best price.

CONTACT OWNER in SEVEN DAYS

12. Discuss sales associates' comments about showings.
13. Present feedback on price and condition.

CONTACT OWNER in FOURTEEN DAYS

14. Call agents; obtain potential buyer and agent feedbacks.
15. Discuss comments with sellers.
16. Review financing possibilities.

CONTACT OWNER in TWENTY ONE DAYS

17. Discuss potential buyers' comments and activity.
18. Discuss market evaluation sales and competition.
19. Discuss price, terms, and condition.
20. Review seller's motivation and urgency to sell.
21. Discuss price adjustment.

CONTINUE TO CONTACT OWNER ON A
WEEKLY BASISUNTIL SOLD

#8   **Exit Guarantee**

When you list your home with us, we take the pressure off of you and put it on us. With our EXIT GUARANTEE, you have the option to cancel the listing at any time.
No hassles and no questions asked!

Here's how it works:

- ✓ You can cancel your listing at anytime with a written notice. (No reason necessary.) (A $50.00 FMLS/MLS fee required)
- ✓ Enjoy peace of mind knowing that your agent is motivated to produce results.
- ✓ Feel confident that everything possible is being done in order to get your home sold.
- ✓ Know that talk is cheap, but a guarantee is priceless!

The reason why [Your Company Name Here] offers the EXIT GUARANTEE is because our business is built on referrals from our past clients. We believe that if a client is unhappy with his agent, he should have the right to fire that agent.

It takes confidence in the way you treat your clients and in the results you can produce to offer this type of guarantee. Only a company that consistently provides superior service and results to its clients would risk offering such a guarantee.

Our goal is to sell your home at an acceptable price and in a timely fashion. Throughout the process, we will ensure that you are comfortable and well-informed. We know that if you are satisfied with our service, you will refer us to your friends and family members. That is what we are truly working for.[7]

_____   _____

Agent   Seller

_____   _____

_____

7 ©2007 Buffini & Company Joe Niego

#9

**Logo
Company
Name
Contact Information
Web Site**

You Have Been in Your New Home for Two Weeks!!

Dear _____,

Congratulations on your new home. We want you to know that we are here if there is anything you need.

As a real estate professional, I set a very high standard for myself, and I am looking for a little help to increase my referral business. A large percentage of my business comes from my past clients. The best compliment you can give me is a referral.

With each referral that you send you will receive a gift card for dinner out. So spread the word to your friends, family, and coworkers.

Sincerely,

Your Name

Your Realtor for Life!

<u>[Your Name]</u> *is never to busy for your referrals!*

If the property is currently listed, please disregard this letter. It is not our intention to solicit another broker's listing.

#10　　　　　**BUYER INFORMATION RECORD**

NAME　　　　　_____

Address　　　_____City　_____　State　_____Zip

Home #　　_____　Bus #　_____

Children's Names

PROPERTY DESIRED

Number Bedrms.		No. Baths		Garage	
Stories		Fireplace		Family R	
Style		Basement		Sq. Ft	
Backyard/ Fenced		Dining Rm		Lot Size	
School District		Location		Age	
Possession By		Price Range		Lender	

Buyers Agency Signed　　　Date

1. How soon do you need to be settled in your new home?
2. How long have you been looking for a home?
3. Have you seen any homes that you have liked? (What did it look like?)
4. If I found the right home for you in 2-3 days, what would you do?
5. Are you prequalified? Would it be ok if my lender called you?
6. How long have you lived in this area?
7. Where do you work?
8. Do you presently own a home?

* Explain to the buyer that if they see a house listed with another broker to call you.
* Explain to the buyer that you can show them all houses listed by all agencies.
* Explain to the buyer that you will be working on their behalf and that offers them valuable protection.

#11   **CONTRACT PROCESSING FORM**

Residential ____ **Nonresidential** _____ **Sale Price $** _____

Property Address: _____ City: _____

Zip: _____

Binding Agreement: _____ Closing Date: _____

Closing Attorney Name: _____ Phone: _____

Earnest Money $ _____ Held By: _____

Earnest Money Deposit Date: _____

Seller's Name: _____ Address: _____

Phone: _____

Buyer's Name: _____ Address: _____

Phone: _____

Selling Agent: _____ Company: _____

Broker Code: _____ Phone: _____

Listing Agent: _____ Company: _____

Broker Code: _____ Phone: _____

Due Diligence Date End_____

Referral Broker:

Company: _____ Fed Tax ID# _____

Address: 4_____

Agent Name: _____ Referral _____% or $ _____

AGENT MUST COMPLETE

____   Is copy of earnest money attached?

____   Earnest money deposited according to terms of contract?

____   Do all forms have all signatures/initials?

____   Do all forms have acceptance dates?

____   Is acceptance date within time limit of offer?

____   Is sellers disclosure attached?

____   If before 1978, is lead-based paint disclosure initialed and included?

____   Is commission agreement attached?

____   Is buyer agency agreement attached?

#12   MOVING WITH CHILDREN

Moving with children can pose additional considerations. It can be a time of uncertainty for the children. Below are some tips on helping your children cope with the move and making them more comfortable with their new neighborhood.

- ✓ Prepare your children for the move and include them when making plans. Get their input on the best way to say good-bye.
- ✓ Take time to show your children their new home, new bedroom, and neighborhood.
- ✓ Involve your children in deciding how his/her new bedroom will be arranged.
- ✓ Get your children an address book and help him/her collect the phone numbers and addresses of his friends, so he can stay in contact with them after the move. Older children can exchange e-mail addresses.
- ✓ Go to school with your children the first few days to help them adjust to their new classrooms and teachers.
- ✓ Aside from school, investigate other activities or organizations your children can participate in around the new neighborhood.
- ✓ Listen to your children's concerns about the move and discuss them with him.
- ✓ Maintain your children's daily routine as much as possible.
- ✓ Moving stress can be more acute with older children; be sure to watch your children for loss of appetite, insomnia, and unexpected mood changes. Consult a doctor or counselor if the behavior persists.
- ✓ Give your children packing duties; set aside a box or two in which they can pack their favorite toys.
- ✓ For safety, arrange to have smaller children stay with relatives or at a day-care during the major part of loading and unloading the moving truck.
- ✓ Bring along travel games or other entertainment for the trip to your new neighborhood.
- ✓ For the moving day, pack an ice chest with plenty of sandwiches, snacks, and beverages.
- ✓ Teach your children your new phone number and address. Make a game out of it—see who can memorize it first or make it into a song.[8]

---

8 Ewebengine.com web source

#13

Logo
Company
Name
Contact Information
Web Site

Let Us Help!

Introducing
Contract/Closing Services
For-Sale-By-Owners

We offer a one-of-a-kind service for sellers who want to handle their own marketing and sale.

For a (TBD) fee we will handle the sales transaction for you

This fee includes:

- ✓ **Experienced professional realtors will write the contract**
- ✓ **Professional lender to preapprove loan obligations**
- ✓ **A realtor handles all negotiations between you and your buyer**
- ✓ **A realtor sets up inspections and negotiates repairs**
- ✓ **A realtor sets up closing and reviews final documents**

Please call [Your Name] at [Your Number] for a free consultation

Consider Your Home Sold When You List with [Your Name].
I am never too busy for your referrals.

If your home is currently listed for sale, please disregard this notice. All information deemed reliable but not guaranteed. Equal Housing Lender.

#14   **Please Sign In**

Name_____

Address_____

City_____State_____Zip_____

Phone (____)_____E-mail_____

What are you interested in? Single Family Home ____ Condo/Townhouse ____ Land ___

Number of Bedrooms ___ Number of Baths ___ Features _____

When are looking to buy? Now ___ Within a Year ___ Just Looking ___ Need To Sell ___

****

Name_____

Address_____

City_____State_____Zip_____

Phone (____)_____E-mail_____

What are you interested in? Single Family Home ____ Condo/Townhouse ____ Land ___

Number of Bedrooms ___ Number of Baths ___ Features _____

When are looking to buy? Now ___ Within a Year ___ Just Looking ___ Need To Sell ___

****

Name_____

Address_____

City_____State_____Zip_____

Phone (____)_____E-mail_____

What are you interested in? Single Family Home ____ Condo/Townhouse ____ Land ___

Number of Bedrooms ___ Number of Baths ___ Features _____

When are looking to buy? Now ___ Within a Year ___ Just Looking ___ Need To Sell ___

****

Name_____

Address_____

City_____State_____Zip_____

Phone (____)_____E-mail_____

What are you interested in? Single Family Home ____ Condo/Townhouse ____ Land ___

Number of Bedrooms ___ Number of Baths ___ Features _____

When are looking to buy? Now ___ Within a Year ___ Just Looking ___ Need To Sell ___

****

Name_____

Address_____

City_____State_____Zip_____

Phone (____)_____E-mail_____

What are you interested in? Single Family Home ____ Condo/Townhouse ____ Land ___

Number of Bedrooms ___ Number of Baths ___ Features _____

When are looking to buy? Now ___ Within a Year ___ Just Looking ___ Need To Sell ___

***[9]

---

9   Reference Old Republic Home Warranty, open house registry, http://toolbox.orhp.com

#15   **Short-Sale Authorization Letter**

Date_____

Loan Company_____

Contact Phone Number_____

To Whom It May Concern:

I am writing you in reference to the property located at _____
_____, loan number of first
_____ and loan number of second _____
_____.I am hereby giving authorization to _____
Agents Name_____, **with** _____ **Real Estate**
Company_____ representative negotiation privileges on my behalf.

Thank you very much for your assistance in this matter.

Name:_____   S.S.#_Last 4 digits_____

Name:_____   S.S.# Last 4 digits_____

Signature _____

Signature_____

#16   # Short-Sale Checklist

Owners' Name(s):_____

Address_____

Mortgage Company Information (including loan number)
Company_____ Loan #_____

Contact_____ Phone_____

REO/Loss Mitigation Specialist Assigned_____

	Contact #_____
Second	Mort. Co. _____
	Loan # _____
	Contact _____/Phone_____
Third	Mort. Co. _____
	Loan # _____
	Contact _____/Phone_____

Owner(s)' Home/Work/Alternate Contact Number/Info:

Name_____ Work #_____

Name_____ Cell #_____

Information from Seller: **Information from Agent:**

___Hardship Letter from Owner(s)   __Copy of Listing Agreement

___Two Recent Bank Statements   __Copy of Listing Agreement

___Two Most Recent Pay Stubs   __Authorization Form

___Copy of Latest Statement from   __Payoff ordered_____

    Mortgage Company   __Amount of payoff_____

___Tax Returns and W-2s or 1099s   __Foreclosure ate_____

___Bankruptcy (yes __ no __)   __Attorney notified_____

If yes, contact information for   __Attorney _____

bankruptcy attorney:_____   __Lender notified_____

    __Sellers Net Sheet/HUD

#17   # Special Stipulations

1) Buyer acknowledges that the sale of the property will not generate sufficient cash to pay off the mortgages on the property and the other obligations of seller with respect to this purchase and sale transaction. This agreement is therefore contingent upon seller's mortgage lenders(s) agreeing to: (1) take a reduced payoff on its mortgage(s) in an amount sufficient such that the purchase price of the property pays off the reduced amount of the mortgage(s), any other liens, judgments, and other encumbrances on the property, the real estate commission(s) owing to the broker(s) and the other expenses of sale for which seller is obligated under this agreement without seller having to pay any additional sums: and (2) release seller from any claim, cause of action, suit, or judgment for the amount of the reduction in the payoff on said mortgage(s). In the event, the mortgage lender(s) do not agree to such reduction at least ten days before closing, either seller or buyer may terminate this agreement without penalty upon written notice to the other party.[10]

2) Buyers and sellers acknowledge that all terms, offers, and conditions are subject to seller's lenders' approval.

3) Buyers and sellers acknowledge that property is being sold *as is* with no repairs.

4) All short sale closings are to be held at [your Attorney Name and Number].

5) Acceptance date will be when the seller's lender accepts contract. All due diligence will start at that time.

---

10 Source GA Assoc. of Realtors SS 516, Short Sale Contingency, copyright 2009

#18　　　　　　　　　**Sellers Net Sheet**

Date:

Owners Names

Address

Sales Price　　　　　　　_____

Real Estate Comm. ?%　　_____

Recording Fees　　　　　_____

Filing Fees　　　　　　　_____

Property Tax　　　　　　_____

Courier Fee　　　　　　　_____

Attorney Fee　　　　　　_____

Estimate Net proceeds　　_____

*Take your sales price and subtract everything else. This gives you your net proceeds

*You need to work with the closing attorney to get these fees. Even though the seller does not pay for the attorney I include it anyway. If you are short you pay!

*Most Short Sales will not pay for closing cost, home warranty or the termite letter.

#19   **LISTING INFORMATION SHEET**

To Be Turned in with All Listings

Agent Name: _____

Property Address: _____ **City:** _____ **Zip** _____

Owner's Name: _____

Owner's Home Phone: _____ **Work:** _____ **Cell:** _____

Owner's E-mail Address: _____

GA MLS #: _____   **FMLS #:** _____

List Date: _____   **Expiration Date:** _____

_____ **Listing Agreement/Seller's Disclosure**

_____ **Signed Listing Agreement**

_____ **Signed Property Disclosure**

_____ **Tax Record**

_____ **Covenants and Restrictions**

_____ **HOA Information**

_____ **Listing Service Input Sheet**

_____ **Home Warranty Ordered**

#20   **OFFER WORK SHEET**

Agent Name_____ Phone #_____

Fax# _____ Web Address_____

Offer Price   _____

Earnest Money   _____

Closing Cost   _____

Closing Date   _____Move Out Days_____

Closing Attorney   _____

Due Diligence Period Days _____Ending Date_____

Appraisal Exhibit/Initials _____

Agency/Brokerage   _____

Material Relationship _____

Seller's Property Disclosure/Signatures _____

(Make sure all *yes* items are explained)

Financing Contingency/Initials _____

Special Stipulations   _____

Subdivision Association Exhibit_____

Financing Cont. Exhibit Loan Type_____%_____

FHA/VA Exhibit   _____

Time Limit Date   _____

Signatures   _____

Acceptance Date   _____

Binding Agreement Date _____

#21 **SETTING UP THE CLOSING**

1) Turn the following documents into your office and ensure all forms are complete.
    a. Contract processing sheet *(see forms #11)*
    b. Contract
    c. Buyer's brokerage agreement (if applicable)
    d. Commission agreement
2) Fax copy of the contract to lender (if yours) and set up closing time
    a. Lender name_____
    b. Loan officer_____
    c. Type of loan_____
    d. Closing cost_____
3) Amendment to remove inspection contingency
    a. Have purchaser set up appointment
    b. Ensure you know the time frame within which it must be completed
    c. Make sure closing attorney has copies of any changes to the contract, including price.
4) Inform the other agent and the customer of the closing time.
5) Fax copy of the contract to closing attorney/ set up closing time/ obtain directions to the closing attorney's office.
    a. Name/Address closing attorney_____
    _____
6) Set up closing folder/order gift.
7) Send directions and utility information to the selling agent and call the seller/ buyer and request that he bring his drivers license to the closing.
8) Call in home warranty if applicable.
9) On the day of closing remove Sale sign, lockbox, and book.
10) Set up information for follow-up; prepare anniversary track sheet (see forms #1)
11) Add to monthly mailing list.
12) Two weeks after closing, mail a post closing letter (see forms #9) and include five business cards for those referrals.
13) Always go to the closing and review the HUD statement for accuracy.

#22

**Logo
Company
Name
Contact Information
Web Site**

Happy Anniversary

Date

Dear _____

Did you know that most home owners cannot tell you what their home is worth?

Do you know the dollar value of your home? I want you to be one of the few who are informed.

A comparative market analysis (CMA) is the only tool that provides current pricing of homes in your home's style and area. With a recent CMA and knowledge of your home's condition relative to others, you can determine an accurate dollar amount for your home.

Enclosed is a complimentary CMA. Please contact me to schedule a time when I can take a closer look at your home's upgrades and improvements and provide you with an in-depth, personalized analysis.

My business card is enclosed; I look forward to hearing from you.**11**

Sincerely,

[Your Name]
Realtor

Your Realtor for Life!

If you have friends or relatives who are considering the purchase or sale of a home, I'd love to be of service to them. So, when you think of these people, just give me a call with their names and business numbers. I'll be happy to follow up and meet their real estate needs.

If the property is currently listed, please disregard this letter. It is not our intention to solicit another broker's listing.

---

11 ©2007 Buffini & Company

#23

**Logo
Company
Name
Contact Information
Web Site**

Date

Dear _____,

INFORMATION ON FILING FOR PROPERTY TAX RETURNS AND HOMESTEAD EXEMPTION

Now is the time for all home owners who acquired property in **[YEAR]** to file for Homestead Exemption.

Homestead Exemption is a way to lower your property taxes.

This is a benefit to you.

Some counties will allow you to file online, while others require you to file at the courthouse in your area.

If I can be of service, please do not hesitate to call. Best wishes for a great year!

We love referrals. Remember me if you hear of anyone buying or selling a house.

Sincerely,

Signature
Realtor

Your Realtor for Life!!

#24   **CREDIT CHECK**

I, _____, give, [Lender Name], with [Lender Mortgage], authorization to examine my credit through major consumer agencies. I understand that this information will be used to evaluate my suitability as a tenant. I further understand that [Lender Name] will not share this information with anyone outside the landlord of said property.

Signed:_____

Print name:_____

Date:_____

#25   **RENTAL APPLICATION**

(Please Print)

Address of property applying for_____

Requested date of occupancy_____

Contingent upon_____

Name: _____Birthday_____

Social Security #_____Marital Status_____

Home Phone #_____Cell#_____Office#_____

Present Address_____

How Long? _____ Reason for leaving:_____

Own_____or Rent_____Payment Per month_____

Name, Address, and Phone Number of Present Landlord

_____

_____

Previous Address: _____

How Long?_____Reason for leaving_____

Owned_____or Rented_____Payment Per Month_____

Present Employer, Address & Phone Number_____

How Long Employed?_____Salary Per Month_____

Spouse Employer, Address & Phone Number_____

_____

How Long Employed?_____Salary Per Month_____

Name, Relationship, and Ages of All Other Potential Residents_____

Pet? No____Yes_____If Yes, Types: _____Inside or Outside Animals

In Case of Emergency, Please Notify_____

I hereby certify that the above information is true and correct to the best of my knowledge and give_____(owner) permission to investigate the information and to obtain a credit report.

I hereby certify that I have been furnished a copy of the lease form to be utilized in the leasing of the property I am applying for and that I understand and agree to the terms and conditions contained therein.

I understand the security deposit for the property for which I am applying is to be paid in full and submitted with this application and is fully refundable in the event this application is not approved but will be forfeited as liquidated damages in the event I withdraw the application after notification of its approval. I further agree that the security deposit cannot be applied as payment of rent, whole or in part, at anytime.[12]

_____   _____

Signature　　　　　**Date**　　　　**Signature**　　　　　**Date**

_____   _____

---

12 Source Jennifer Sims, lender

ORDER CD'S

To order the forms on CD send $14.95, this includes shipping charges, to Vicky Keeton 3300 Hamilton Mill Rd., Suite 102-176, Buford, Ga. 30519. Be sure to include your mailing instructions.

The CD includes customizable forms as presented in this manual, plus samples of just sold postcards, just listed postcards, custom flyers, exceptional features notations, and more. Please allow 30 days for delivery.

You can contact Vicky at vkeeton@windstream.net with any comments or questions.

Note: This manual originated in Georgia. Some of the material may not be suitable for usage in your state but all of the ideas and suggestions should lead you to success.